To My Readers

This book is meant to give you the basic understanding of the "Rosin Technology." All of the information contained inside is gathered from my personal experiences and preferences in researching and developing presses for this "fast growing industry."
Reading this article and understanding the concept of how it works, is the first step in deciding how to move forward in this industry.
The keys to success are simply, heat, pressure, good material and mastering "The art of the Squish"

Doing things slightly different or with a twist is what makes you and your product special. I challenge you to go out there and seek out or grow that special breed and press it out. It is fact, that if you have a good product and you make good decisions, you are more likely to succeed.

In the world of Rosin, as a patient, it's about health, but as a business, it's all about the bottom line.

CONTENTS

ACKNOWLEDGMENTS

I acknowledge that I wrote this book based on my experiences, and months of research. All of my research is based on common knowledge and common sense and all the pictures included were taken by and are property of Domeless.com

All persons involved in the making of this book would like to remain silent and much thanks go out to those of you that opened up your farms and provided the much needed research materials.

1
WHAT IS ROSIN

What is Rosin and where does it come from? A simple Google search will show that there is more than one type of Rosin and many more uses than that. In this article we will be discussing marijuana Rosin. Marijuana Rosin (just called Rosin from this point on) is produced by heating the oils contained in the flowers to the melting point and then using pressure to squeeze the now fluid oils away from the plant matter. The process can be simple and small or massive and complex, depending on the amount of materials to be processed at one time and the press

Pressed Flowers & Rosin

needed to accomplish such a task. Although the process of pressing cannabis has been around for many centuries, only now due to new legislation are we able to practice these techniques freely. Aside from the laws changing, we're growing flowers in our basements, bathrooms, and closets that our ancestral botanist could

Rosin on dabber

1

only dream of. Our generation is breeding and growing some real potent flowers. The rise of Rosin can "almost" be contributed to the fall of (BHO) (Butane Honey Oil). Due to the combined aspects, flammability, ease of access, and simply just not thinking, lots of people were getting injured dispensing the butane (in some cases,) inside the home. The process was looked at by Law Enforcement, and was deemed to be comparable in risk to cooking Methamphetamines and the process was outlawed in most areas. That and the need for a better and Organic process brings us back to our roots and the renowned hash press is reborn as the notable "Rosin Press." The cool thing is, you should be able to squeeze out between 95-100% of whatever oils are in your flowers, just by using heat and pressure.

Rosin Flow
Using Mr.Rosin Press

Note: By removing the oils from plant matter it's now easier for exact dosing, packaging and or just about anything else you can think of not to mention the ease of consumption without the excess potential cancer causing carcinogens.

Trichomes 500x Mag

Rosin 500x Mag

2
PSI VS. LBS
Pressure vs Force

This page is to help you understand how force and PSI are used when considering a press. It gets confusing generally because when you buy a press, jack, or scale, it comes with a force rating not a Psi rating. This is standard because usually when you use a press in a shop type surrounding, you will be using adapters with different sizes allowing

Common Press Adapter

you to determine your own psi based on your needs. Here is some more info to help you better understand what's going on.

Force = LBS
PSI = Pressure/Square Inch

150 lbs / 1.5 psi

150 lbs / 150 psi

The bottom of a 10" x 10" Box has a 100 square inch surface. By dividing 150lbs by 100 square inches, you get 1.5 psi, but if the same box were to be placed on its corner, it would be distributing all its weight to a single point. (Assuming the corner is 1 square inch), the PSI will then be 150 PSI.

Note: To further increase the psi, you can reduce the perimeter size in half to double the psi and you get a total of 300psi or by going the other way, you can decrease psi by increasing the perimeter; for example, a 2 square inch perimeter would result in 75 psi.

What does all this mean to me?

When pressing your materials, you should be using the

smallest perimeter possible. Ideally you will be making "pucks or cylinders" with your materials. Just keep in mind that the larger the perimeter of the puck the more the pressure will be distributed throughout it. For instance, if you wanted to press more material at

Turn trim into cylinders and Press!!

one time, the perimeter would be small, and the puck will become taller and start to resemble a cylinder.

It's important to remember that the psi is determined by the amount of force, and the perimeter size of the material being pressed not the size of the surfaces doing the pressing. Force is applied where the perimeter of the material makes contact. Often times it's best to make cylinders since you're able to run more material at one

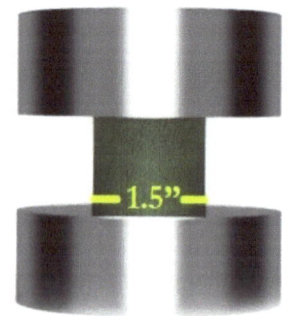

1.5"

1.5" Puck = 5g - 10g Flower

time. Depending on the material, the height, and density, the cylinder will compress and may expand outward on the surface effectively reducing the overall psi by redistributing it over the perimeter of the now pressed materials.

The picture below shows how the psi is reduced as the puck expands under 1140 lbs. force.

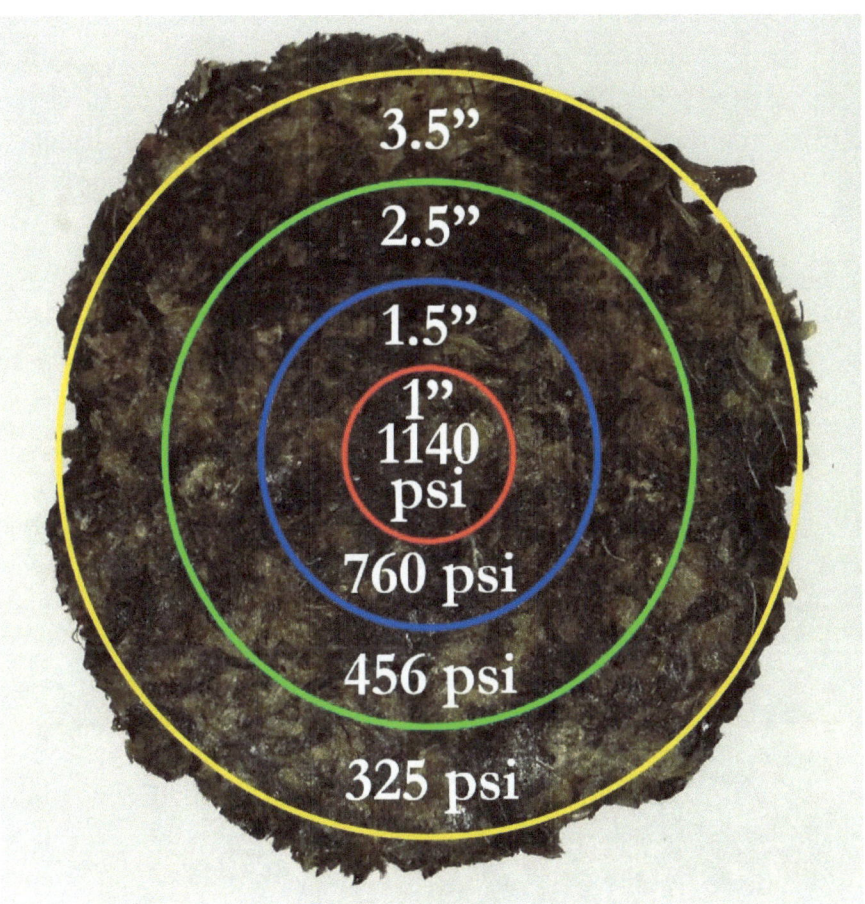

Note: This has nothing to do with the PSI of your air compressor. As the "Psi" from an air compressor flows into whatever press your using, the pressure is converted to Lbs. "force" in the cylinder and redistributed through the ram.

Psi/Force Conclusion:

Whether you're about to purchase a hair straighter or a 20ton press with "Dual Heated Plates", it's my conclusion that 150lbs of pressure per square inch is sufficient to squeeze the oils away from the material once the material is up to temperature. So if you're using a hair straightener, make sure it can withstand all the pressure you're going to be putting on it. If it's a 1ton or more, from your local freight tools or similar, you have more than enough force/psi to press out more than a pound at a time, "assuming if you have the correct setup" *. Chances are you're more concerned about the plant matter pressing out the sides of the plates, breaking or ripping your parchment, or even breaking your bags when pressing sift. One key is not to press too hard and or to use less material for that size of plates.

Pressing Hair Iron with C-Clamp

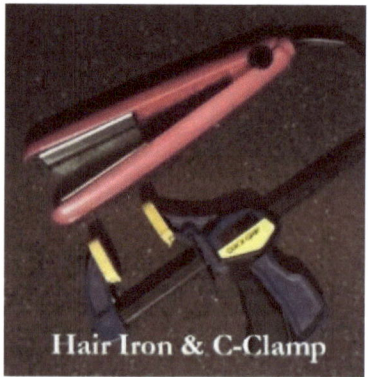

Hair Iron & C-Clamp

Note: It's "almost" never acceptable to press on a padded surface, as this will reduce your psi by design. For example, the rubber of a T-shirt press is meant to "give way" in case a seam, button, pocket or collar is pressed, so that the decal will still be pressing on a flat surface. You can usually place a thin sheet of metal on the pad so the surface won't flex. If it's a -shirt press were talking about, the main thing to remember is, it's a T-Shirt press, not a rosin press…

3
PRESSING TEMPS AND TIMING

Rosin Temp	Viscosity
40F -60F	Most rosin will be like glass at this temperature.
Room Temp	"Stable" Rosin might be solid or can be like soft taffy.
90F-200F	Rosin will become more fluid at higher temps.
200F+	Thermal degradation occurs and rosin begins to darken.
250F-275F	Rosin will begin to boil – Different temps for different strains. Decarboxylation occurs.

Below is a chart to record your temps & times based on what you have learned and your experiences. I have filled in a few examples. **Hash** and **Kief** will have different times based on the oil content.

PRESS TIMES

Material Weight	190F	200F	210F	220F	230F
1 Gram Flower	2:00				
1 Gram Sift		:35-:50			
5 Grams Flower					1:15
5 Grams Sift					:50-1:30

"The Business End of The Squish"

Aside from applying pressure, the temperature is the single most important key to pressing the oil out. The goal of the temperature is to melt the trichrome bulbs into a fluid so that they can collect and then be pressed away from the plant material. Remembering that the Rosin will start to degrade at higher temperatures, that's where the timing comes into play. You want to make sure the temperature is high enough to melt the oils, but not to harm them. Another thing to consider is the amount of materials being pressed, and the amount of time it takes to transfer the heat entirely throughout all of said material.

The conclusion is that, by increasing the amount of material to be pressed you also increase the time needed to press all the oil out.

Note: Consider the amount of time it takes to melt butter or cheese, it's not instant, and the time taken differs in the amount of product to be melted. A "stick or block" of butter or cheese will take longer to melt rather than if it were shredded or sliced. Primarily, due to its surface area.

Remaining oil will be noticable on the puck after pressing

As for the timing, "at first press" I don't put a limit on it. Imagine you stopped pressing because you were going off of a set time, you might leave some of that precious oil in the material you're pressing. After several months of research, I have found that by simply listening to the oils bubbling, combined with watching the oils flow, you can accurately remove all 95% of all the oils in the puck. This process is usually the first step to be taken when running samples or getting ready to run a large amount of the same material. If you're going to do a large run, you should keep track in a log so you can compare against other strains or for whatever reason you might have. At the very least, you can make an educated decision when obtaining or cultivating your next batch of materials to process.

Note: It should be your goal to press out at least 95% of the oils on the 1st press. Generally, the 2nd press will contain some other plant juices and be darker in color. It's best not to mix the two together unless you really don't care. Then who cares! Right?

Note: The higher the temperature, the faster the oils will flow, and for lower temps, the oils will take longer to squeeze out. As well, the higher temp will likely produce a darker oil than oil pressed out at a lower temperature.

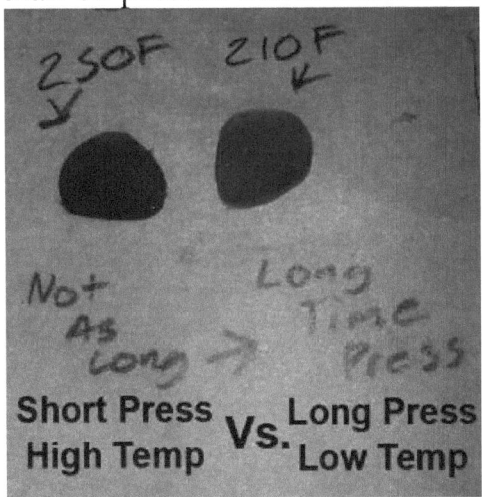

It's my personal preference when pressing 1.5" round pucks with about 5 grams flower, to press at about 230 F.

This I feel gives me a hot enough temp to melt the oils in the flowers without taking forever to do so. If you're just pressing a couple grams at a time, 215F seems to work well.

I also enjoy, when my friends come over to Sesh, to press it out at 200 F, since nobody is in any real hurry. However, if I was paying someone to sit there and press for me, I might want the temp to be higher as to get the job done faster. You will find that everybody has their own personal preferences. Everybody's situation and strain to be pressed is different. With that said its clear there is no 1 perfect temp or press time but, there is something for every situation.

GG Rosin From Flower

Not All Flowers Were Grown to Be Pressed

Low Yield Flower   Vs.   High Yield Flower

4
OIL CONTENT OF MATERIALS
"If you want it to press out, you have to put it in..."

By far, the biggest factor in making materials "squirt", is the oil content of the materials themselves. If there's no oil on the flowers, then there is no oil to press out.
If you have 20% tested material, when you press 1 gram of it, you should get at least 19% oil back, if not the full 20%.
When testing for oil content using a press, as long as your material is pressed properly, you should always get an accurate "oil content" result, within 1-2%.

How To Test Your Yield
There is 1,000mg in 1g
If you press 1 gram of flower and say you get .2g or 200mg, That is equal to 20% yield. I use my cell phone to calculate most of my percentages but here is a basic cheat sheet for the round numbers anyway.

Pressed Rosin - Yield Percentages Chart

Weight	30%	25%	20%	15%	10%
1g	.3g	.25g	.2g	.15g	.1g
2g	.6g	.5g	.4g	.3g	.2g
3g	.9g	.75g	.6g	.45g	.3g
4g	1.2g	1g	.8g	.6g	.4g
5g	1.5g	1.25g	1g	.75g	.5g
10g	3g	2.5g	2g	1.5g	1g

In my pursuit of pressing juicy flowers and talking to the gardeners that produce them, they all have different methods and or tricks to growing the biggest, fattest, terpiest trichome's, but they all insist on 1 thing. Basically it all comes down to the light. The more intense the light throughout the plant partnered with the perfect environmental controls and a killer strain bred for its oil content, you'll have the perfect press materials.

Type of Grow	Average oil content
Outdoor	8% to 25%
Indoor	10% to 28%

In my testing while pressing samples from different gardeners and types of grows, there was usually a noticeable difference in trichome head size from the top cola's and the bottom popcorn flowers. Handling and trimming also appeared to slightly affect the content on some dryer samples.

Moisture content is very important to the flowers wellbeing and also when determining how to move forward with extraction. You might place excessively dry flowers directly in a screen and press it out or you might choose to sift it first. Both options are acceptable.

It should be noted that when pressing above 212F, the moisture content from the materials being pressed will boil and turn to steam during the press. These are, in my opinion, the bubbles we witness coming out as the oils flow. And yes, I suppose that some of the bubbles can be from the decarboxylation of the oil.

In a rare occasion I witnessed part of 1 g. of flower exploding out the front of the press due to steam build up from pressing at 197C by mistake. That's 386F. It was an amazing "Fail!"

5
CONCENTRATES
FROM CONCENTRATES
Pressing Sift

By far the best yields I have ever seen have come from pressing dry sift and or ice water extract. The fact that the majority of the plant matter has been removed means it should contain more oils by weight compared to the flowers where the oils originated. Every situation is different, but if I had the option, I would press "untrimmed" flowers straight out of the cure room.
If you're just buying the sift to process it, just make sure it's fresh or you're likely to press out some dark oil with a less than appealing taste.

Note: When pressing out concentrates using screens, it's most important to use a screen that is smaller than the screen('s) used to collect the sift. If you use a screen the same size or larger than the original collection screens, the plant matter of the materials you're pressing will press right through the mesh and mix with your rosin. I'm sure this is not what you're after. To avoid this situation, make sure to have a variety of micron screen sizes on hand.

Pressing sift:
It's okay to use lower temperatures to separate the oils but use caution when pressing hard as you don't want to press any of the plant matter though the screen into your rosin pile. Also if using a nylon screen, you don't want to blow it out by over pressing it. If you have this problem, try using less sift in your pouch.

6
MESH/SCREEN SIZES

There are a lot of sizes of micron, so only the most relevant are listed below. Also different manufactures use different thread sizes in their mesh screens. Because of this, the actual hole sizes vary among manufactures.
When it comes to screens and micron sizes, there's actually a science to it, but I will keep it simple.

Mesh	Micron	
400	37	Super small mesh size
210-200	70-74	The smallest sizes
140-120	100-120	The medium sizes
100-80	150-170	The largest sizes
50	300	Very large Size

Sizes are approximate, you should ask your retailer for exact numbers.

Screen Basics

The main thing to remember when pressing sift using a screen, is to use a screen smaller than the sift particles. For example, if the screen used to collect the sift was 100-170 microns. You would then use 75-90 micron screen to press with since the holes are smaller and will capture the plant matter when pressed.

If you're interested in learning more, please research "Absolute rating vs. Nominal rating for filters."
It's also worth looking into "thread counts" and "diameters of the treads" being used, along with differences in US, Euro, and Asian thread counts.

Sewn vs. Folded

You can buy or sew your own pouches, but I tell you what, after a little practice folding and more than a few blowouts I am now, quite the pouch folder.
Give it try, I'm sure you'll get it!!!

Nylon / Poly vs. Stainless Steal

Nylon / Polyester	Stainless Steel
Inexpensive - Pro	Expensive - Con
Can break easily - Con	Very Strong - Pro
Uses limited amounts of materials - Con	Can use excessive amounts of material - Pro
One time use - Con	Reusable - Pro

7
THE PROCESS
Basic Steps to Pressing:

1. Preheat your press.

2. Compress your flowers or pack your sift

3. Place your materials in a piece of parchment

4. Place your parchment on the pressing surface making sure your materials are in the center or at least far enough away from the edge of the surface so that the plant matter won't squeeze out of the parchment or press plates, under all the pressure.

5. While pressing, listen and watch for all the oils to press out. As the temperature rises and the oils start to bubble, you should be able to hear it and or see the oil puddle expanding. At a certain point only heat bubbles will be coming out and its time to hurry and cool the parchment on a room temperature surface. This will help to prevent the oils from degrading.

6. When you're ready, it's time to collect the rosin and get it ready for storage. It's best to use a multi tool dabber that has a flat scraping surface on one end and a point tip on the other to remove any particles that are unsightly. I personally enjoy seeing the hairs and itty bitty particles. It's like having pulp in my orange juice. With that said, it's not for everybody. When collecting, its best to avoid the area where the materials were pressed as this area has most likely lost its hydrophobic properties during the press. (If this concerns you, there are many debates online that you can follow.) After collecting a significant amount of Rosin on your dabber, its best to remove it onto the parchment paper you intend to store it on.

7. After collecting all of your Rosin, you can now press it flat, weigh it and label it for reference.

A
PUCKING IT UP
Puck Making Technique

The easiest and most time efficient way to "Puck It Up", that I have found, is to use a shot glass to make 1.5" pucks for the "Mr. Rosin Press" or I use a tea cup to form 3" pucks for a larger press. I'm sure there are better things out there to use but a shot glass or tea cup always seems to be available wherever I'm about to press.

1. Size up some parchment paper to (1) fit the bottom of the glass and (2) to cover the sides.

2. Place the small piece on the bottom and roll the long piece into a circle and line the side of the glass.

Rosin

Rosin

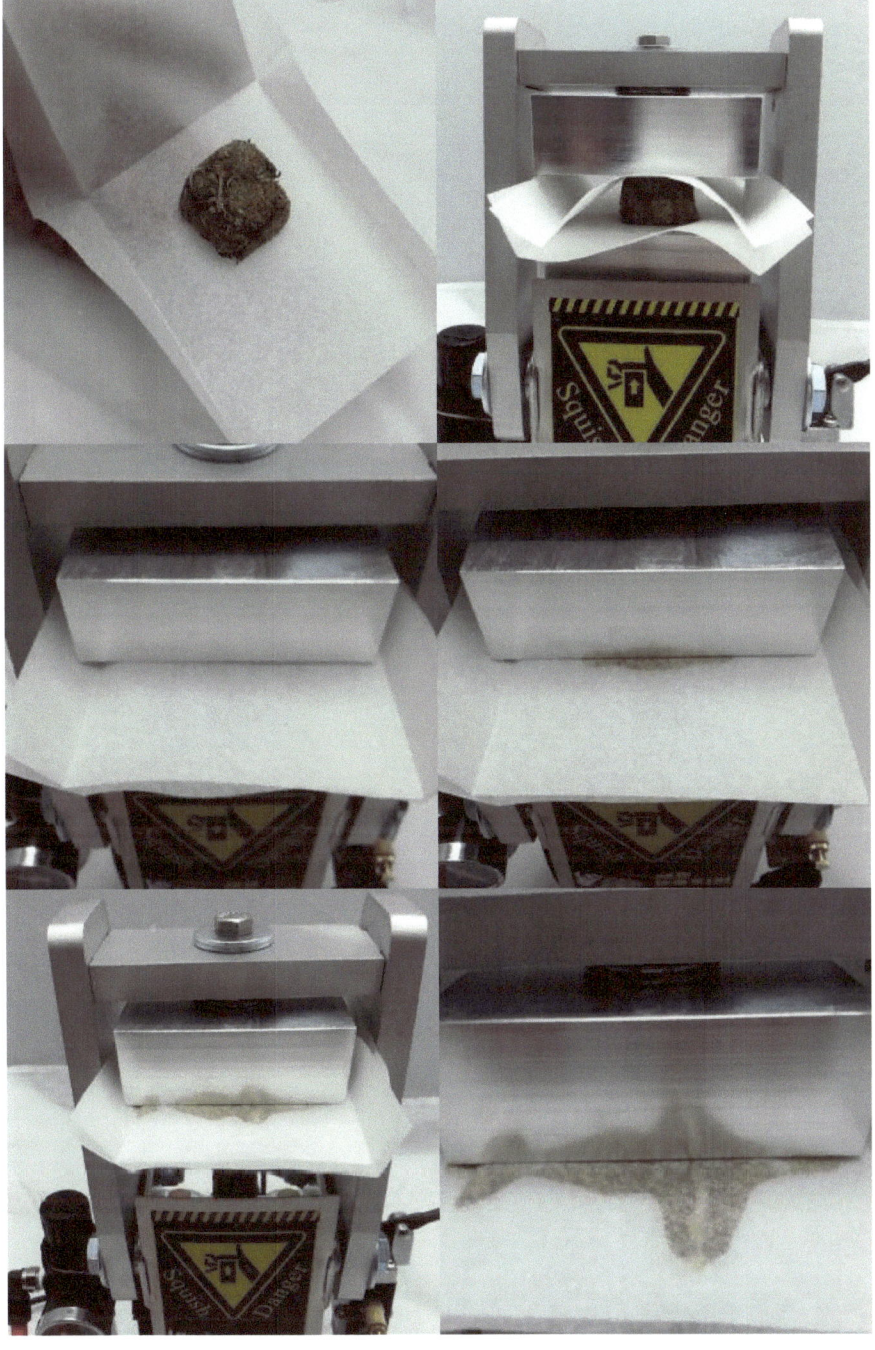

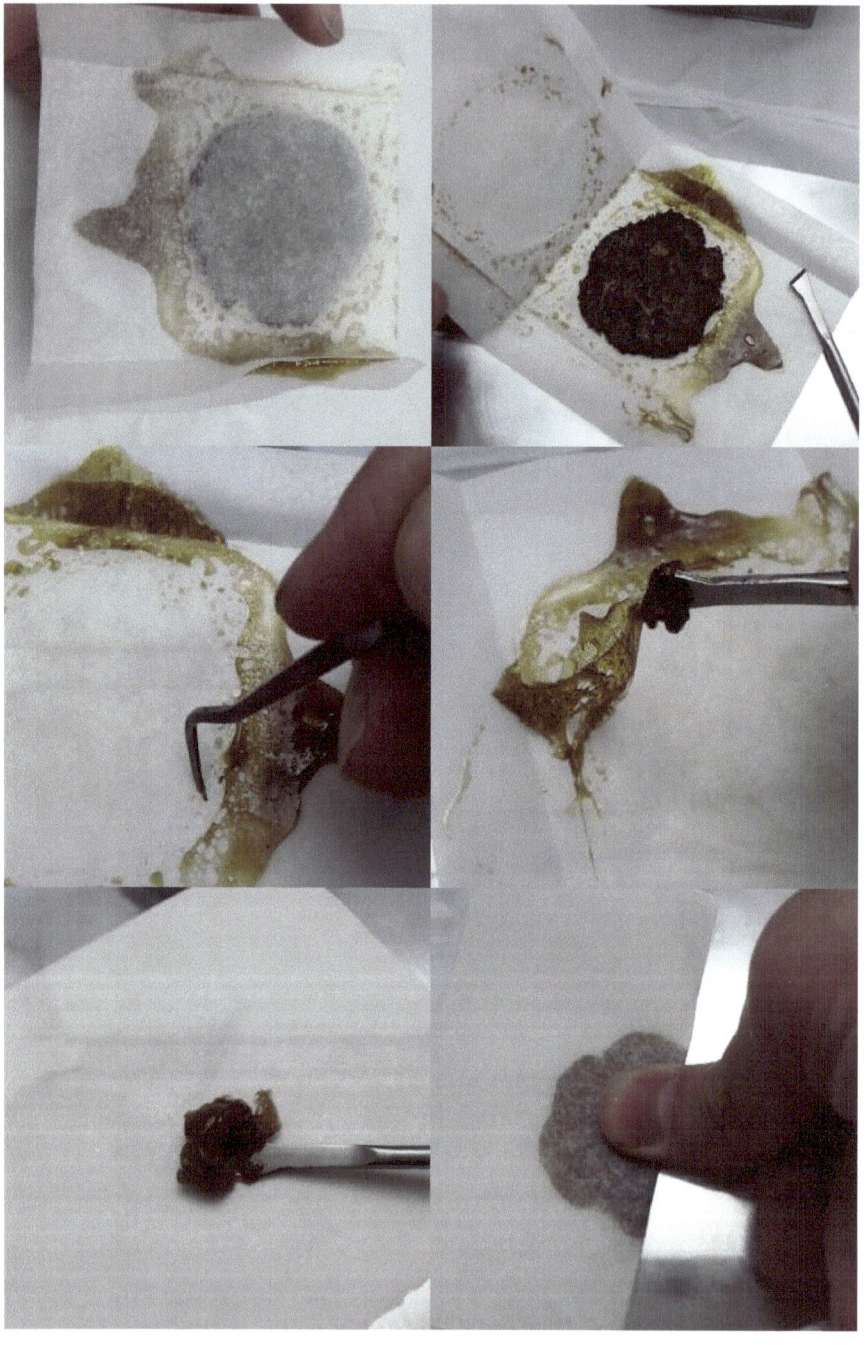

MrRosin Press

The coffee machine sized, portable rosin press, packs the perfect punch. It provides
1140 lbs force and runs on compressed air.

Comes with 3.5" press plates in either round or square, based on your preference. Designed and manufactured in Seattle, WA by Domeless.com
Distributed by **www.MrRosin.com**

20 Ton Press
RosinPlates.Net
& Truck Scale

Sponsored By www.RosinPlates.net

Sorry for not including more information regarding the process of pressing "Hashes and kief's" in this volume. There is much information to provide, so look out for a volume 2.

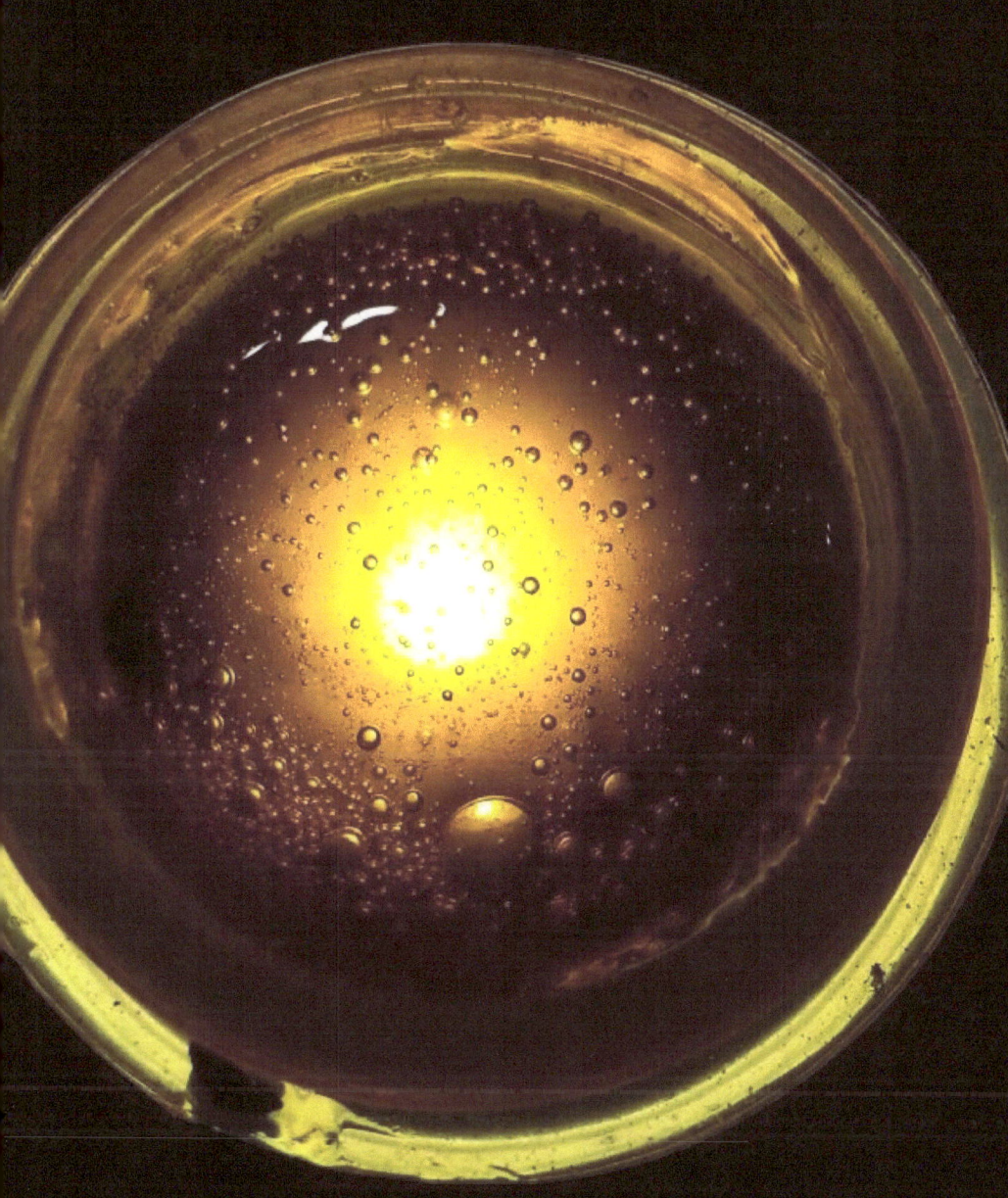

While I was in the process of writing this book
I made a couple breakthroughs in press design.
These pictures are a result of the process and
represent the future of the industry.

www.ingramcontent.com/pod-product-compliance
Lightning Source LLC
Chambersburg PA
CBHW050920290526
45792CB00002B/834